IDEOLOGY AND INFORMATION

CREATIVE EDUCATION

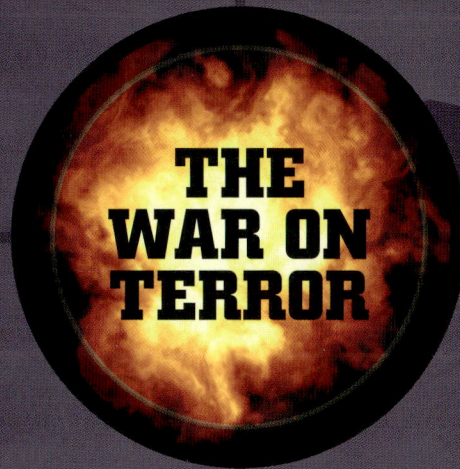

THE
WAR ON
TERROR

BY TERESA WIMMER

Published by Creative Education
P.O. Box 227, Mankato, Minnesota 56002
Creative Education is an imprint of The Creative Company
www.thecreativecompany.us

Art direction by Rita Marshall
Design and production by The Design Lab
Printed by Corporate Graphics in the United States of America

Photographs by Corbis (epa, Petra/epa), Getty Images (AFP,
Mark Downey, Dutch School, Joseph Eid/AFP, Douglas Graham/
Roll Call, Ramzi Haidar/AFP, Dia Hamid/AFP, Mahmud Hams/AFP,
Julian Herbert, Saeed Khan/AFP, Yuri Kozyev, Shah Marai/AFP,
Toby Melville-Pool, John Moore, Mandel Ngan/AFP, NYC Office
of Emergency Management, Karim Sahib/AFP, Karl Schumacher/
AFP, Mario Tama, Mark Wilson), iStockphotos (Andrew Robinson,
Sculpies)

Library of Congress Cataloging-in-Publication Data
Wimmer, Teresa.
Ideology and information / by Teresa Wimmer.
p. cm. — (The war on terror)
Includes bibliographical references and index.
Summary: An examination of the differences in religious and
political beliefs between Western nations and Islamic extremists, as well as the ways in which information is shared and
manipulated.
ISBN 978-1-60818-099-8
1. War on Terrorism, 2001-2009. 2. Terrorism—Religious aspects—Islamic countries—Juvenile literature. 3. Terrorism—Political aspects—Islamic countries—Juvenile literature. 4. Islamic countries—Politics and government—Juvenile literature.
5. Islamic fundamentalism—Juvenile literature. 6. Ideology—
Islamic countries—Juvenile literature. I. Title. II. Series.

HV6431.W56633 2011
909.83'1—dc22   2010033842

CPSIA: 110310 P01387

First Edition
9 8 7 6 5 4 3 2 1

TABLE OF CONTENTS

A photographer accompanies a 2001 gathering of fighters in the Northern Alliance, a collection of Afghanis who opposed the Taliban.

In the late 1980s, a conflict rooted in terrorism began to rear its head on a global scale. This strife pitted Islamic fundamentalists, radical religious **militants** springing primarily from nations in the Middle East, against the countries and culture of the Western world. Spilling across parts of four decades, this conflict—which came to be known from the Western perspective as "The War on Terror"—grew from bombings and guerrilla combat into the first large-scale war of the 21st century, marked by the infamous events of September 11, 2001, and intensive military campaigns in the countries of Afghanistan and Iraq.

At the root of the War on Terror are differing core sets of beliefs, or ideologies—those held by the democratic nations of the West, and those held by believers in Islam, or Muslims. Religion has played a central role in the formation of these ideologies, as have historical differences between the cultures of the West and the Middle East. As the first major conflict of the 21st century, the War on Terror has been monitored by and reported on incessantly by media outlets around the world, making information available instantly worldwide. Both sides of the conflict have also employed various means of communication to broadcast their message to the world, making the war not only a struggle for victory on the battlefield but in the hearts and minds of people as well.

CHAPTER ONE

ALLEGIANCE TO ALLAH

Today, Islam is the second-largest religion in the world (after Christianity), with about 1.66 billion followers. It is also the world's fastest-growing religion. Most believers in Islam are concentrated in the Middle East, which is more than 90 percent Muslim, and Asia. For devout Muslims, Islam is more than a religion—it's a way of life. Muslims pray to Allah (God) daily, submit themselves to Him by following Islamic law and commandments laid out in the holy book the Qur'an (or Koran), and believe they will be eternally rewarded if they follow Allah's commands.

At the heart of the Islamic faith is the idea of *tawhid*. Because Muslims believe Allah is the one true God, His rule extends to all aspects of creation. Thus, Islam is inseparable from society, law, and government. It is the duty of all Muslims, as Allah's agents on Earth, to create a just community in which all members are treated with fairness and respect. In Qur'an 49:13, Allah said to Muslims that He "created you from a single soul, male and female, and made you into nations and tribes, so that you may come to know one another."

Muhammad—the prophet to whom Allah revealed the message of the Qur'an in the seventh century A.D.—was the last in a line of prophets that included Abraham, whom Christians and Jews also revere. Yet

The Qur'an has not changed since the seventh century, yet interpretations of the holy book have varied widely among the world's Muslims.

although Islam, Christianity, and Judaism are all **monotheistic** religions, Islam differs significantly from Christianity and Judaism in many ways. Muhammad preached a return to the pure message of Islam (submission to Allah) which was originally given to Abraham, believing this message had been distorted throughout the centuries as Judaism had given rise to Christianity. Islam's departure from the centuries-old paths of Christianity and Judaism has created tension among the three religions since Islam's founding.

From the beginning, Muslims have not seen political affairs as a distraction from spirituality but as central to their religion. Throughout history, every Islamic government has been held up to the laws and ideals spelled out in the Qur'an, and if its leaders were found to be corrupt or exploitive, every effort had to be made to overthrow them. For centuries, Islamic empires governed a large portion of the known world. However, beginning in the 16th century, Europeans began to take over many Muslim-held territories in southeastern Europe and the Middle East. In 1918, after World War I (1914–1918), the weakened Ottoman Empire, the last of the

This map from 1606 shows the geographic sprawl of the Ottoman, or Turkish, Empire when it was near the height of its power.

SONS OF ABRAHAM

Abraham had two sons named Isaac and Ishmael. Isaac, the younger, was the forerunner of Christianity and Judaism, while Ishmael, the older, was the forerunner of Islam. Because Ishmael was born to a servant in Abraham's household, not to his wife, he and his mother were banished to the desert. There, Allah promised to make Ishmael's descendants a great nation. While Christians and Jews honor many prophets, Muslims believe that Muhammad was the only prophet to whom Allah revealed his word. This was the beginning of Islam's separation from Christianity and Judaism.

MUSLIM BROTHERHOOD

In the 1920s, Egyptian thinker and teacher Hassan al-Banna founded the Muslim Brotherhood, a group that advocated incorporating scientific advancements from the West with a return to pure Islamic law. Appalled by what he saw as the "looseness" in Western society—including gambling and a lack of religious devotion—al-Banna urged the use of nonviolent jihad to bring about a revival of Muslim power and restore Islamic governments to Middle Eastern nations, such as Egypt and Saudi Arabia, that had formed partnerships with Western governments.

great Islamic empires, was disbanded and its remaining territories divided up and claimed by Western allies such as France and Great Britain. This disintegration was a devastating blow to the ummah, or worldwide community of Muslims. The fall and division of the Ottoman Empire—along with the creation of Israel in 1948 as a Jewish homeland—helped set the stage for **jihad** movements in the Middle East.

According to traditional Islamic teachings, jihad can take two forms: greater jihad and lesser jihad. Greater jihad refers to the internal struggle each person experiences to do what is right and become a better Muslim. Lesser jihad is the struggle against enemies to defend oppressed peoples and establish justice. Neither form advocates using violence, but Islamic fundamentalism, which gained momentum in the mid-1900s, focused on an extreme form of lesser jihad, embracing violence as part of the effort to restore purist Islam to the Middle East.

In response to the growing power and global influence of Western nations after World War I, the governments of some Middle Eastern countries, such as Turkey, chose to adopt **secular** forms of government. Islamic fundamentalists took offense to such governments, believing that all Muslim countries needed to return to their Islamic roots. Some fundamentalists used nonviolent means to affect this change, such as creating religious groups to bring about social reform and challenge political parties. However, a new, radical form of fundamentalism began to grow in popularity in the 1960s. It was then that an Egyptian thinker and teacher named Sayyid Qutb called those committed to Islamic rule "good" and those opposed to it "evil." He advocated forcibly removing "corrupt" (which usually meant pro-West) leaders of Muslim countries, such as Saudi Arabia and Iran, and destroying the nation of Israel, which received great support from the West.

In the 1980s and '90s, this new Islamic radical movement, which came to include groups such as al Qaeda, Palestine's Hamas, and Lebanon's Hezbollah, was influenced heavily by Qutb's writings, especially his 1964 book *Milestones*. These groups believed it was every Muslim's duty to wage jihad—which they interpreted to mean "holy war"—against Western nations by attacking them and the Muslim governments that cooperated with them. A defining moment for Islamic jihad occurred in 1981, when Ayman al-Zawahiri, who later became a leader of al Qaeda, and other jihadists assassinated Egyptian president Anwar al-Sadat for making peace with Israel.

When the United States stationed troops in Saudi Arabia—a U.S. ally—as protection from Iraq during the Persian Gulf War in 1991, Islamic radicals were outraged at the thought of the West occupying Islam's holiest cities of Mecca and Medina, which lie in Saudi Arabia. Extremist groups decided the time had come to send a strong message to the West—especially the U.S.—that it must end its involvement in the Middle East or

Egyptian president Anwar al-Sadat, U.S. president Jimmy Carter, and Israeli prime minister Menachem Begin (left to right) in 1978 peace talks.

RETURN TO WAHHABISM

Wahhabism—the most conservative form of Islam—was founded by cleric Muhammad ibn Abd al-Wahhab in the 18th century. Followers, called Wahhabis or Salafis, believe theirs is Islam's only true path, and they reject the worship of Islamic saints and consider all other forms of Islam illegitimate or corrupt. For decades, Saudi Arabia has been the world's biggest promoter of Wahhabi ideals. Osama bin Laden, who grew up in Saudi Arabia, acted upon his radical Wahhabi beliefs in urging Muslims to attack the "corrupt" governments of Western and Middle Eastern nations.

An aerial view of the collapsed World Trade Center on September 15, 2001; barely three weeks later, America would officially be at war.

face dire consequences. In 1998, five prominent Islamic jihadists, including al-Zawahiri and Osama bin Laden, vowed to wage jihad against all Americans, civilian and military, until all Islamic holy cities were liberated and all Western forces departed from the Islamic world forever. "Al Qaeda believed," said American author and professor Mary Habeck, "that the United States, as the greatest representative of 'unbelief,' had to be struck a stunning blow ... to frighten the U.S. government into submission."

On September 11, 2001, a group of 19 al Qaeda hijackers flew planes into the World Trade Center skyscrapers in New York City and the **Pentagon** in Washington, D.C. A fourth hijacked plane crashed in a Pennsylvania field after the passengers revolted. The hijackers saw themselves as brave "knights" who would—by their courage and heroism—become **martyrs** and inspire the ummah to follow their lead in jihad. The Western world saw them as terrorists.

CHAPTER TWO

FREEDOM FOR ALL?

With the attacks of "9/11," the U.S. realized the full capability of Islamic terrorists, and many Americans found themselves in a state of shock. They had never before witnessed an attack by foreigners on home soil, and they struggled to understand why people would hate the U.S. so much that they would kill nearly 3,000 innocent civilians. To seek answers, many people went to their local place of worship. For the majority of Americans, this meant a Christian church.

When drafting the U.S. Constitution, America's founding fathers—many of whom belonged to various Christian denominations—made sure to state that no single religion would be established as the national religion, and that religious matters should be kept separate from political matters. This stands in stark contrast to the religion of Islam, which teaches that Allah should be the center of true Islamic government and that religious and political matters are therefore inseparable. Christians believe in the trinity of the Father, Son, and Holy Spirit (one God in three forms) and acknowledge many prophets; to Islamic fundamentalists, there is only Allah and Muhammad. Christians thank God for sending his son Jesus Christ to save all people from their sins. Muslims, however, believe people are born as blank slates and that through doing kind acts and living devoutly, each person can become his or her own savior.

The 9/11 attacks compelled many Americans to embrace their own religious faith, such as these Catholics in New York City's St. Patrick's Cathedral.

DIVINE PATHS

Even though Muslims consider the teachings of the Qur'an to be the one true path to becoming closer to Allah, most believers also respect the teachings of Judaism and Christianity. Historically, Muslims have believed that the holy message delivered to Christians and Jews, although different from that of Islam, is divine in origin and have respected their beliefs and holy books. They call Christians and Jews *Ahl al-Kitab* ("People of the Book") and declare that they are to be protected by Islamic governments.

Although the U.S. supported Afghan militants during the Soviet War in Afghanistan, it attacked some of those same fighters as enemies in 2001.

Americans and other countries of the Western world pride themselves on their **democratic** societies and freedom of speech. They believe that freedom for all people is essential to making it possible for individuals to seek happiness and success, which will in turn benefit society as a whole. People in the U.S. generally identify themselves first as Americans—their ethnic or religious background usually is of secondary importance. The majority of Arab Muslims, however, identify themselves first as members of the ummah, then in terms of their tribal or ethnic background, then as a citizen of their particular country. This places much more emphasis on each person as a member of a collective whole, along with the responsibilities that entails, rather than as an individual.

Although the U.S. government had become concerned about the growing number of jihadists in the Middle East following the **Soviet War in Afghanistan**, the public, as well as many officials, did not consider an attack on U.S. soil possible. After 9/11, however, government officials, led by president George W. Bush, felt compelled to take unprecedented action. For the first time, all commercial U.S.

flights were grounded in the days following 9/11. Airport security was tightened in the U.S. and around the world, and American baggage screeners were required to be employees of the federal government. As part of the National Strategy for Homeland Security outlined by the Bush administration, the newly formed Department of Homeland Security combined government agencies—such as those dealing with customs, immigration, and emergency management—in order to better protect American citizens from attacks. U.S. Customs and Border Protection officers detained and questioned hundreds of people going into and out of the country.

Bush also took more liberties than most prior U.S. presidents by making the executive branch of government able to take action and institute laws without always consulting Congress. In November 2001, Bush signed an order authorizing the use of **military tribunals** to try non-citizens who he had "reason to believe" were affiliated with al Qaeda or sponsored terrorism. Vice president Dick Cheney, secretary of defense Donald Rumsfeld, and other members of the Bush administration believed that the traditional tools and methods of law enforcement, such as obtaining search warrants and conducting federal trials, were not enough when dealing with al Qaeda, a stateless enemy that blended in with the civilian population. As American law professor David Cole noted, the administration "repeatedly invoked not only the actual attacks of September 11 but the specter of an even

Donald Rumsfeld, George W. Bush, and Dick Cheney (left to right) emerged as the three most prominent figures in America's War on Terror.

ANTHRAX SCARE

Shortly after 9/11, envelopes containing anthrax—a kind of deadly bacteria that reproduces in warm, moist places such as lungs—began appearing at American television stations and U.S. Senate offices, including the office of Senate majority leader Tom Daschle. Many people initially feared that terrorist organizations such as al Qaeda were resorting to biological warfare. By the time the mailings stopped at the end of 2001, the anthrax had killed 5 people and infected at least 17 others. In 2008, the **Federal Bureau of Investigation (FBI)** focused its investigation on an American scientist, who soon afterwards committed suicide.

more devastating future attack with chemical, biological, or nuclear weapons to justify previously unthinkable security measures."

With the aid of the media, the War on Terror largely became a conflict of ideals and **rhetoric**. In Bush's 2002 State of the Union address and other public announcements, he frequently referred to the concept of "good versus evil" and phrases such as "wanted: dead or alive" in America's hunt for al Qaeda terrorists. Analysts offered different explanations for the motives behind the terrorists' assault on the U.S. Some pointed to America's occupation of Saudi Arabia during 1991's Persian Gulf War and its alliance with Israel. Others, including Bush, argued that people fear and envy what they do not

have—in this case, the freedoms, democracy, power, and wealth of the U.S. "Why do they hate us?" Bush asked Congress in a September 2001 address. "They hate our freedoms ... of religion, ... of speech, ... to vote and assemble and disagree with each other." Whereas bin Laden and his followers believed it was their duty to defend Islam, drive **infidel** invaders out of the Middle East, and return Islamic nations to their former glory, Bush soon made clear through his speeches that he believed it was his duty to free the world of terrorism and establish Western-style democracies in more nations. In October 2001, the U.S. and a **coalition** of allied nations invaded Afghanistan to attack al Qaeda. Ideologies had become war.

IN GOD WE TRUST

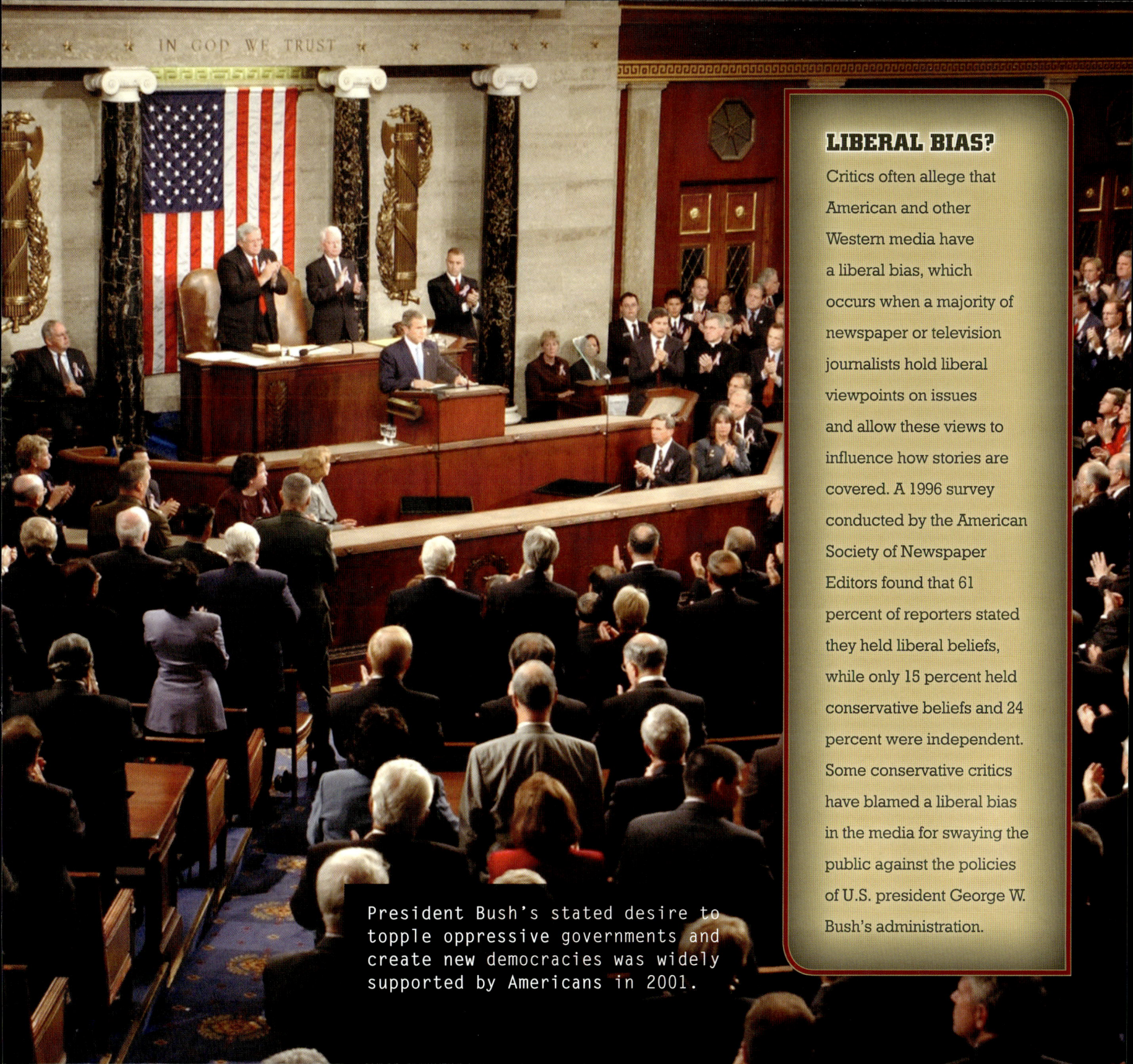

LIBERAL BIAS?

Critics often allege that American and other Western media have a liberal bias, which occurs when a majority of newspaper or television journalists hold liberal viewpoints on issues and allow these views to influence how stories are covered. A 1996 survey conducted by the American Society of Newspaper Editors found that 61 percent of reporters stated they held liberal beliefs, while only 15 percent held conservative beliefs and 24 percent were independent. Some conservative critics have blamed a liberal bias in the media for swaying the public against the policies of U.S. president George W. Bush's administration.

President Bush's stated desire to topple oppressive governments and create new democracies was widely supported by Americans in 2001.

CHAPTER THREE

THE MEDIA TAKES OVER

In the years after the 9/11 attacks, as all-out war unfolded in Afghanistan and Iraq, al Qaeda used the media in different ways to promote its ideology and to justify its attacks to the ummah. In the 1990s, al Qaeda members, especially bin Laden, had recorded messages and sent them to radio and television stations such as Al Jazeera—a prominent, independent Arab news network—for broadcast to the Middle Eastern public. Internet technology in the 2000s, however, made it easier for bin Laden and other al Qaeda leaders to put videos online, allowing the group's message of jihad to instantly reach Muslims around the world. In these messages, bin Laden assured Muslims that al Qaeda was doing the right thing with its assaults against the West and that its actions, even the most violent, were necessary and even

Osama bin Laden

The Qur'an, studied by Muslims from a young age, represents all that Muhammad learned about Allah through 23 years of revelations.

LEARNING BY HEART

The prophet Muhammad could not read or write, so each time he received a revelation from Allah, he memorized the words. Then he recited them to his companions, who also learned the words by heart and wrote them down. Today, many Muslims still try to memorize the Qur'an as a way of praising Allah. A person who knows the entire Qur'an by heart is known as a *hafiz* and is highly respected.

approved by Allah. Although most Muslims denounced the violent actions of al Qaeda and other fundamentalist groups as defying the peaceful principles of Islam, most nonetheless understood the rationale behind them.

Al Qaeda broadcast messages frequently in the first years after 9/11. Demonstrating an ease in front of the camera, bin Laden employed a media strategy tailored to video clips and prime-time news **sound bites**, giving brief, straightforward speeches that were easily understood by even poorly educated people. Many of his videos were edited to show graphic images of dead or injured Afghan civilians—suggesting that they had been harmed by U.S. forces—interspersed with footage of bin Laden himself. On October 7, 2001, in bin Laden's first videotaped appearance after 9/11, he gave a speech while sitting on the ground at the mouth of a cave, dressed in traditional Afghan clothes—a presentation that was meant to demonstrate how his being stripped of all worldly goods and hiding out in Afghanistan's inhospitable mountains separated him from America's excess.

The media coverage of the Iraq War also helped to promote al Qaeda's ideology of jihad. Al Qaeda's calls for violence against the West found an audience among the poor and middle-class people of the Middle East, especially those from the **madrasas**, where jihad is glorified. In the spring of 2003—just after a military coalition led by the U.S. and Britain had invaded Iraq and toppled the oppressive government of president

Iraq fell quickly in 2003; within three weeks of the invasion's start, U.S. troops and Iraqi citizens were removing images of Saddam Hussein.

I DIVORCE YOU

Divorce, or *talaq*, is not taken lightly by Muslims. According to sharia (Islamic law), a husband must declare divorce three times to make it irrevocable. In 2003, the Malaysian government overruled a decision by an Islamic cleric that allowed the declaration of divorce to be sent by text message over a cell phone. When children are involved in a Muslim divorce, the mother is usually given custody of boys under age 9 and girls under 12. Custody of older children is awarded to the father.

IRAQI GOVERNING COUNCIL

The Iraqi Governing Council—a group of Iraqis appointed by the U.S.-led Coalition Provisional Authority (CPA) in July 2003 to help revive Iraqi self-rule and write a temporary Iraqi constitution after the fall of Saddam Hussein—was originally made up of 25 members from Iraq's various ethnic and religious groups. Three of those members were women. One of them, Aqila al-Hashimi, was shot to death by Hussein loyalists in September 2003. Another male council member, Ezzedine Salim, was killed by a car bomb in May 2004.

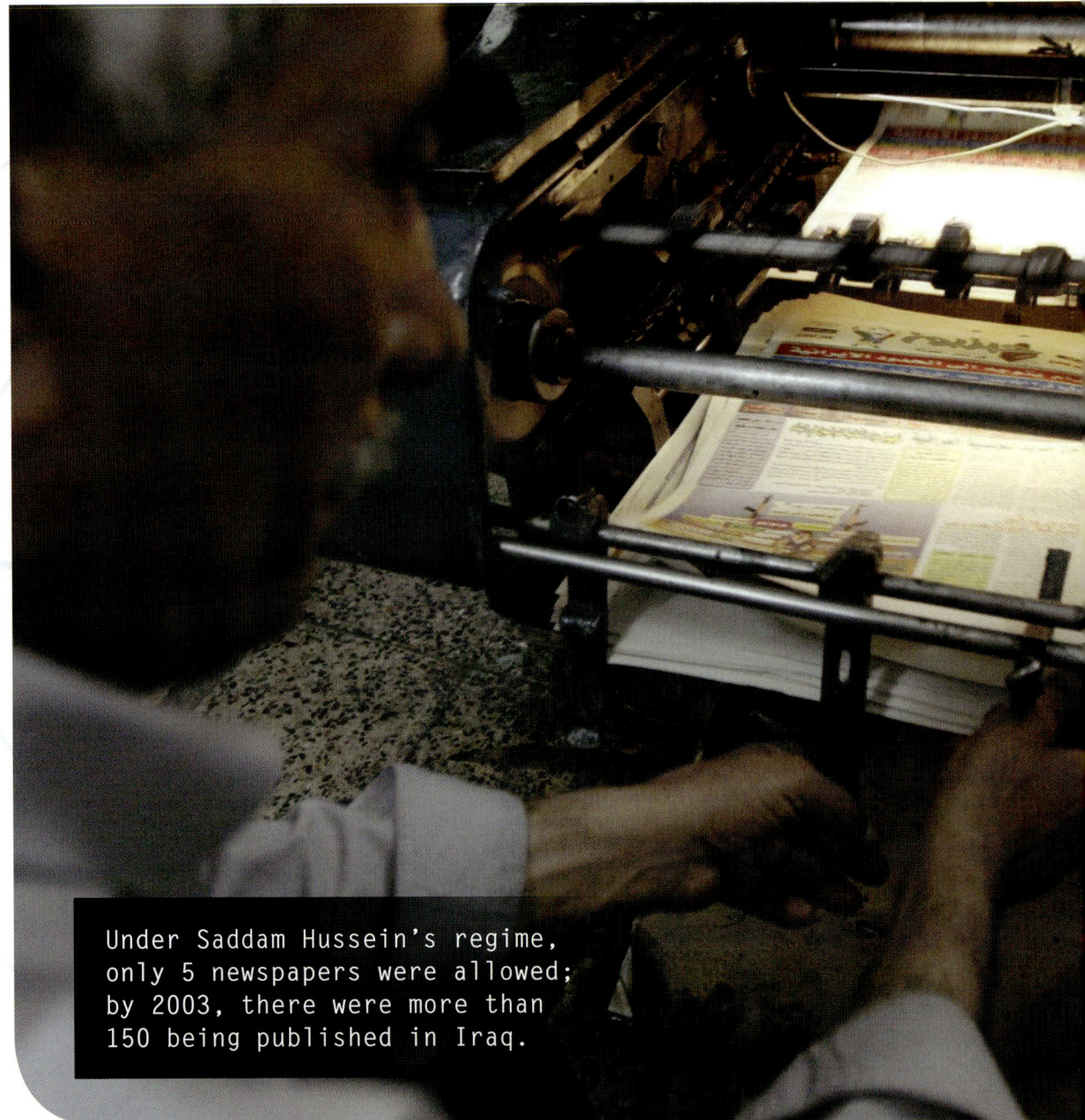

Under Saddam Hussein's regime, only 5 newspapers were allowed; by 2003, there were more than 150 being published in Iraq.

Saddam Hussein—Iraqi **insurgent** groups began to take over the media assets of Hussein's old regime and set up their own newspapers and radio and television stations. They used these media sources to speak directly to the Iraqi people and to urge violent resistance to the coalition. The wars in Afghanistan and Iraq allowed al Qaeda and other jihadists to continue their **propaganda** that the U.S. wanted to kill Muslims, control Islamic states, and exploit the area's resources. Exposed to this repeated message, many Muslims could not help but wonder—after U.S.-led forces had invaded two Muslim countries—if the War on Terror was really a war on Islam.

However, when Abu Musab al-Zarqawi, the leader of al Qaeda in Iraq, made war in the spring of 2003 not only against the foreign invaders but also against fellow Muslims, Middle Easterners and even other jihadists rejected his brutal violence. Al-Zarqawi took advantage of the chaos created by the Iraq War to launch vicious attacks against coalition forces and to urge Sunni Muslims to attack Shia Muslims in Iraq. Sunni leaders do not believe that Shia (or

Shiites) are true Muslims, and al-Zarqawi embraced this notion to the extreme. As American author and military historian Frederick W. Kagan explained, "He ... delighted in killing Shia, whom he saw as intolerable 'rejectionists,' who had received the message of the Koran and rejected it."

Along with the killing of coalition troops, al-Zarqawi directed the bombing of Shiite shrines and the murder of Shiite leaders and ordinary citizens. After Middle Eastern television stations broadcast images of the atrocities suffered by innocent Iraqis, bin Laden and al Qaeda's second-in-command, Ayman al-Zawahiri, commended al-Zarqawi's bravery and violence against coalition forces in Iraq but cautioned him that his continued persecution of Shiites may make him lose popular support. When an estimated 34,000 Iraqi civilians were killed in 2006, many at the hands of al-Zarqawi and other al Qaeda terrorists, and nearly 20 percent of the population fled the country for fear of religious persecution and death, the

Abu Musab al-Zarqawi

30

The violence between Shiites and Sunnis in Iraq, marked by numerous bombings, became so intense that many people termed it a civil war.

A RELIGION DIVIDED

Muslims are divided into two main sects, or factions: Sunni and Shia. This split occurred after the prophet Muhammad's death in 632 A.D. Muslims who became Sunnis believed that the leader of Islam after Muhammad should be elected based on his ability. Muslims who became Shiites believed that the religion's new leader should be someone from the prophet's family. Today, Sunnis make up more than 80 percent of Muslims worldwide.

majority of Muslims rejected al Qaeda's radical ideology—especially against fellow Muslims—and called for an end to the violence.

In 2006, Sunni tribal leaders, weary of the violence brought by insurgent attacks, began to retaliate against al Qaeda in Iraq. They formed tactical alliances with coalition forces in exchange for arms and money, creating a partnership that made al Qaeda in Iraq much weaker. As Muslim tolerance for al Qaeda declined, al-Zawahiri and bin Laden broadcast more videos and Internet messages designed to re-energize its jihadist supporters worldwide. In one such video, bin Laden addressed the American people with a message in which he vowed to continue to target the U.S. and other Western nations. "We fight because we are free men who do not slumber under oppression," he said. "We want to restore freedom to our nation, and just as you lay waste to our nation, so shall we lay waste to yours." Around the symbolic date of September 11 every year, al-Zawahiri or bin Laden also gave addresses to people in the Middle East that provided a review of the balance of power between al Qaeda and its adversaries and were intended to mobilize al Qaeda's supporters.

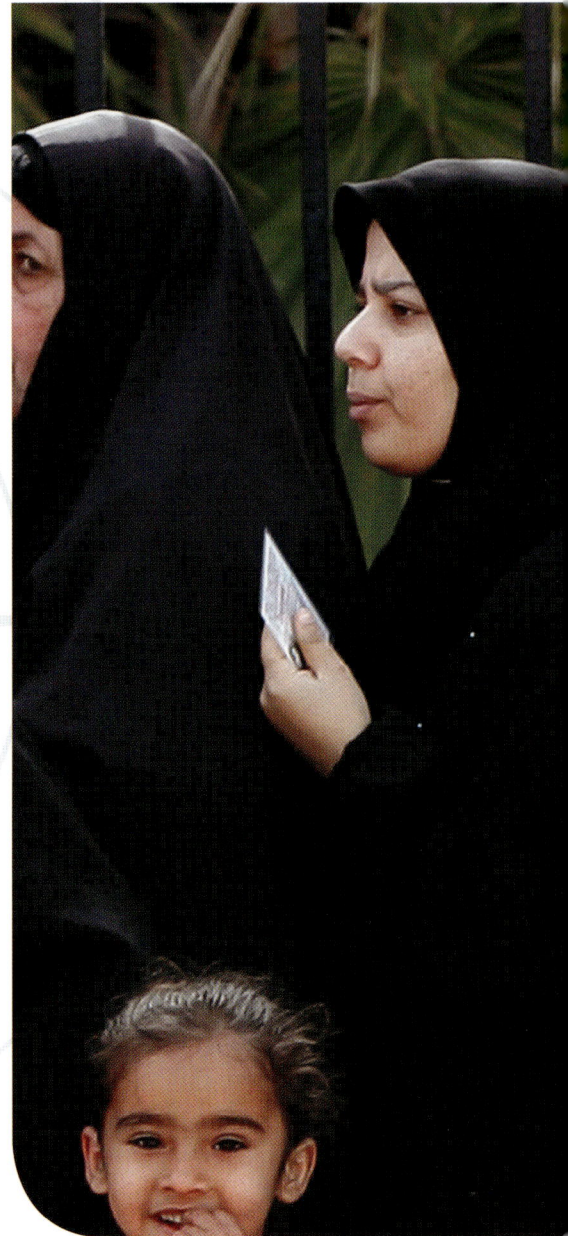

DEATH THREATS

In the run-up to Iraq's January 2005 elections, held to choose members of the new Iraqi parliament, Abu Musab al-Zarqawi declared war—not only on Shiites and the West, but on democracy itself and all who sought to enact it. His al Qaeda followers distributed posters and handbills and circulated Internet messages warning the Iraqi public that to vote was to risk death. Despite these threats and bombing attacks at polling places, Iraqis showed their desire for democracy when 60 percent of registered voters went to the polls, and the election was regarded as mostly free and fair.

Iraqi women, defying the threats of al Qaeda, line up to vote in Basra, a city in the southeastern corner of the country, in January 2005.

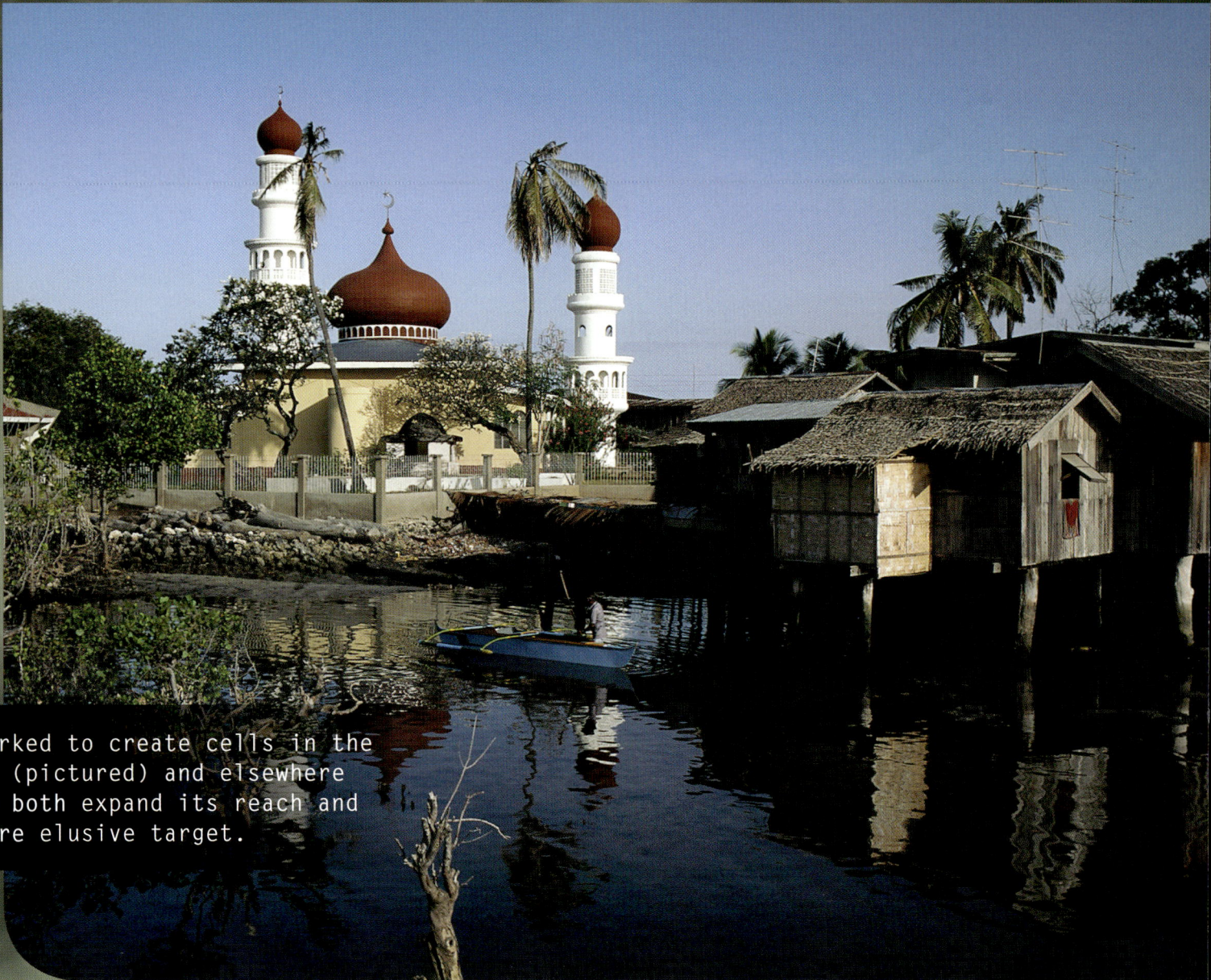

Al Qaeda worked to create cells in the Philippines (pictured) and elsewhere in order to both expand its reach and become a more elusive target.

By 2009, al Qaeda had become much less **hierarchical**. Coalition attacks in Afghanistan had forced al Qaeda's top leaders into hiding, and the organization was forced to run its operations through smaller al Qaeda-affiliated cells, which had grown to number about 50 worldwide by 2010, in such countries as Algeria, the Philippines, and Indonesia. In addition, bin Laden, al-Zawahiri, and other top leaders used al Qaeda's media network, al Sahab, to reach out to people in countries such as Pakistan, where a sharp rise in insurgent attacks and the presence of an unstable, pro-democratic government created a new recruitment base for their jihadist message. In addition, al Qaeda and the Taliban produced thousands of CDs and DVDs promoting messages of continued violence against the West and sold them in the bazaars of Pakistan and Afghanistan for a few pennies each, which allowed its message to reach everyone.

RULES FOR LIVING

The Qur'an gives Muslims guidelines about many aspects of daily life, from legal processes to food. If a new law is needed to deal with modern developments or events, Muslim scholars debate the issue and try to find an answer based on their knowledge of the Qur'an and the Sunna (the record of Muhammad's life and sayings). Food that Muslims are allowed to eat is called *halal*; forbidden food is called *haram*. Most meat is *halal* if it is killed in a particular way and dedicated to Allah, but pork and pork products are always *haram*.

CHAPTER FOUR

HEARTS AND MINDS

As the War on Terror dragged on, the endless media reports began to take a toll on Western audiences. Internet news sites broadcast photos of hostage beheadings at the hands of terrorists such as al-Zarqawi, and news reports gave daily updates of military personnel killed in suicide bombings, as well as the continued elusiveness of top-ranking terrorists. The onslaught of bad news eventually led many Westerners to question their leaders' military strategies and motives for prolonging the conflict.

Although the majority of British citizens supported the U.S.-led invasion of Afghanistan in response to 9/11, they were much less supportive of the invasion of Iraq in 2003. Before the Iraq War began, some military and foreign policy experts had warned that the U.S., Britain, and their allies might become trapped in a **quagmire**, similar to the one the Soviets faced in Afghanistan in the 1980s. Despite these warnings, President Bush and British prime minister Tony Blair decided to proceed with the invasion to rid the world of the threat posed by Saddam Hussein and his weapons of mass destruction (WMD)—chemical, biological, or nuclear weapons that are capable of killing large numbers of people. However, in the summer of 2004, after Hussein's government had fallen, a thorough search revealed that Iraq

President Bush found his most stalwart international ally in British prime minister Tony Blair, who pledged his full support to the coalition.

GULF WAR SYNDROME

After U.S. combat veterans returned home from the Persian Gulf War in 1991, medical professionals monitored their health. The soldiers had been exposed to many toxic chemicals from sources such as smoke, pesticides, and dust from depleted uranium (the radioactive element used in making nuclear weapons). Within months, many of these soldiers began to suffer from symptoms such as lung problems, muscle pain, fatigue, and memory loss. Collectively, these symptoms became known as Gulf War syndrome.

Two years after the 2004 Abu Ghraib abuse scandal, the U.S. military would transfer control of the infamous prison to Iraqi authorities.

did not possess any chemical or biological weapons, nor did it have any plans to acquire them. This revelation made many people in both the U.S. and Britain mistrust their leaders and question their rationales for war.

Scandal soon deepened this level of distrust. In April 2004, the television program *60 Minutes* broadcast images of U.S. military personnel apparently abusing prisoners in Baghdad's Abu Ghraib prison. The media had also run stories alleging detainee abuse at the hands of U.S. guards and interrogators at Cuba's Guantánamo Bay detention center. These revelations embarrassed and angered many Americans. Bush publicly apologized for the abuses and promised that those individuals responsible would be brought to justice. But the damage was already done and

served only to escalate many people's opposition to the war. In cities in both the U.S. and Britain, demonstrators—carrying signs with such slogans as "Many Voices, One Plea: No War in Iraq"—held rallies urging their governments to end the war.

As it faced mounting public pressure, the Bush administration was also accused of having missed the opportunity early in the Iraq War to establish an effective, far-reaching, and democratic media in Iraq—a voice that might have promoted America's message of freedom in an effort to win the hearts and minds of the Iraqi people. Coalition authorities had set up the Iraqi Media Network, overseen by the **Office of Reconstruction and Humanitarian Assistance (ORHA)**, in April 2003. However, because the coalition chose to concentrate its financial resources on military operations, the network was hindered by little funding, broken equipment, and damaged studios.

Immediately after coalition forces captured Baghdad in April 2003, the major networks of the Arab nations, including Al Jazeera, Al Arabiya, and Al-Alam, hired many of the best-known and most experienced Iraqi media specialists to broadcast in Iraq for salaries five times what ORHA was able to pay. Most of these networks took largely anti-American positions on the Iraq War and had their correspondents spotlight every questionable action and magnify every mistake made by the coalition. Such biased media coverage deepened some Iraqis' mistrust of the coalition forces that occupied their cities and caused chaos through urban combat against terrorists and insurgents.

As violence in Iraq continued in 2006, and as regrouping Taliban militants began to launch more bombing attacks against coalition forces in Afghanistan in 2007, many people in the U.S. and Britain remained concerned about new terrorist attacks yet paid less attention to news coming out of the war. Although bin Laden continued to give globally broadcast messages on each 9/11 anniversary prior to his death in May 2011, his messages became less and less noteworthy in the West. In the immediate aftermath of 9/11, many Americans had paid attention when media sources warned them of terrorist threats using the Homeland Security Advisory System's five-color scale, which ranged from green (low risk) to red

In the most conservative regions of the Islamic world, women wear full-body veils behind which even their eyes are concealed.

OPPRESSION OR HONOR?

One of the most common pictures that Westerners have of a Muslim woman is of her body fully covered by a veil except for her eyes and hands. The veil's original intent was to shield women from unwanted advances from men and to protect their honor. Although some countries—such as Iran under the ayatollah Ruhollah Khomeini—forced Muslim women to wear a veil or face punishment, many women today do not consider wearing a veil to be oppressive. Rather, they see it as a symbol of their commitment to Islam.

TALIBAN RULES

When the Taliban, an Islamic extremist group, came to power in Afghanistan in 1994, it began imposing strict laws. Some of these rules involved denying women an education, forcing women to wear **burkas** and men to wear beards, stoning women to death for not having a male escort in public, and imprisoning Afghanis who did not fast at appropriate times or pray five times every day. The Taliban's violent enforcement outraged many Afghan citizens, but most were afraid to speak out against the group for fear of being killed.

Although U.S. president Barack Obama promised swift U.S. military withdrawals, the upheaval in Afghanistan caused him to commit more troops there.

(severe risk). However, as time passed, the American public—which had become accustomed to seeing the terror alert level at orange (high risk)—began to largely ignore the alerts. And when no more attacks occurred on home soil, they paid even less attention to news about bin Laden. Nevertheless, al Qaeda remained a threat to the U.S., as National Counterterrorism Center director Michael Leitner warned the American public in January 2010. "We know with absolute certainty," Leitner said, "that al Qaeda and those who support its ideology continue to refine their methods to test our defenses and pursue an attack on the homeland."

After replacing George W. Bush as U.S. president in January 2009, Barack Obama—a former senator who had opposed the Iraq invasion in 2003—followed up on a campaign pledge to remove all U.S. combat troops from Iraq by September 2010, even while committing 30,000 additional troops to the coalition effort in Afghanistan, where the Taliban remained an elusive yet dangerous presence. Although the violence seemed to be subsiding in Iraq by mid-2010, the situation in Afghanistan remained precarious. The country's vast, mountainous landscape hindered the coalition's mobility and pursuit, and the newly elected, democratic Afghan government, led by president Hamid Karzai, was plagued by allegations of corruption—most notably that government officials accepted bribes from Afghan drug lords. These developments served to undermine the coalition's goal of making Afghanistan a free and safe place for Afghan citizens. The Taliban attempted to perpetuate the message that coalition forces were interested in creating a "puppet" government that could be influenced by the West. This compelled coalition forces to devote themselves not only to combat but also to winning the trust of Afghanis and proving their commitment to reconstructing a free and more prosperous Afghan society.

Although the War on Terror has produced many unforgettable images of violence—from the destruction of the World Trade Center in New York to firefights in Afghanistan to suicide bombings in Iraq—at its core, the war is a conflict of beliefs and information. Muslim extremists have waged "holy war" in the name of a radical version of Islam and have broadcasted accusations of Western corruption in order to justify their acts of terrorism. Governments of the West have promoted notions of "good" versus "evil" and justified invasions of the Middle East with promises of establishing new democracies and thereby new freedoms. And all of it—bullets, bombs, and propaganda—has been covered by the media like no conflict before, making for history's first 24-hours-a-day war.

Thousands of Muslim pilgrims performing hajj pray around the Kaaba—Islam's most sacred site—in Mecca, Saudi Arabia, in 2009.

THE FIVE PILLARS

Islam consists of five pillars—*shahada*, *salah*, *zakat*, *sawm*, and *hajj*—that Muslims must follow. Shahada is the profession that there is no God but Allah. All Muslims must perform salah, or daily prayers. Muslims must pay zakat, or an annual tax, to help poor and less-fortunate Muslims. Sawm—intended to symbolize Muslims' purification—is the fasting that Muslims participate in during the month of Ramadan. Lastly, all Muslims are required to undertake a pilgrimage, or hajj, to the holy city of Mecca at least once in their lifetime.

burkas — loose garments covering the entire body, with a veiled opening only for the eyes

coalition — an alliance of individuals or groups who join together for a common cause

democratic — describing a form of government in which the leaders are elected by the people; the term also describes social equality of the individuals in a society

Federal Bureau of Investigation (FBI) — a governmental agency of the U.S. that investigates federal crimes within America and guards against potential crimes, including terrorist plots

hierarchical — describing a system of people or things ranked one above another, with the most prominent or powerful at the top

infidels — people who do not accept a particular religious faith; it is a term especially used by Muslims as a reference to people who do not believe in Islam

insurgent — describing fighters who partake in a revolt or uprising against a government or ruling force

jihad — a holy war waged by Muslims as a religious duty against people who do not believe in Islam

madrasas — religious schools used for teaching Islamic theology and religious law

martyrs — people who sacrifice something or die for their religion or beliefs; in the world of Islam, the word "shahid" is used for Muslims who die while fulfilling religious commandments or waging war in the name of Islam

militants — people who use aggression or combat in support of a cause

military tribunals — military courts organized in time of war to try offenses by individuals who are not subject to trial by a court-martial

monotheistic — pertaining to the belief that there is only one God

Office of Reconstruction and Humanitarian Assistance (ORHA) — a department established by the U.S. government in January 2003, intended to act as a caretaker administration in Iraq until a democratically elected government could be created

Pentagon — a huge, five-sided building near Washington, D.C., that is the headquarters of the U.S. Department of Defense

propaganda — information, ideas, or rumors that are methodically spread in order to help or harm a person, group, or movement

quagmire — a difficult or precarious situation that is very difficult to resolve or escape

rhetoric — persuasive or elaborate language that can be seen as insincere or empty

secular — being void of religious ties or affiliations

sound bites — short statements, often taken from a longer speech, that are broadcast over the radio or television, usually as part of a news program

Soviet War in Afghanistan — a war from 1979 to 1989 in which the invading Soviet Union attempted to establish a pro-Soviet government in Afghanistan but was ultimately forced out by Muslim fighters

ENDNOTES

Armstrong, Karen. *Islam: A Short History*. New York: Random House Modern Library, 2000.

Cole, David. *Justice at War: The Men and Ideas That Shaped America's War on Terror*. New York: New York Review Books, 2008.

Habeck, Mary. *Knowing the Enemy: Jihadist Ideology and the War on Terror*. New Haven, Conn.: Yale University Press, 2006.

Jones, Seth G. *In the Graveyard of Empires: America's War in Afghanistan*. New York: W. W. Norton, 2009.

SELECTED BIBLIOGRAPHY

Kepel, Gilles, and Jean-Pierre Milelli, eds. Translated by Pascale Ghazaleh. *Al Qaeda in Its Own Words*. Cambridge, Mass.: Belknap Press of Harvard University Press, 2008.

Napoleoni, Loretta. *Insurgent Iraq: Al Zarqawi and the New Generation*. New York: Seven Stories Press, 2005.

Riedel, Bruce. *The Search for al Qaeda: Its Leadership, Ideology, and Future*. Washington, D.C.: Brookings Institution Press, 2008.

Shultz, Richard H., and Andrea J. Dew. *Insurgents, Terrorists, and Militias: The Warriors of Contemporary Combat*. New York: Columbia University Press, 2006.